in, against, beyond corona

IN, AGAINST, BEYOND CORONA

what does living through the corona crisis in South Africa reveal to us?

Mark Butler
with:
Cindy Dennis, Phiwa Xulu, Zodwa Nsibande, David Ntseng, Graham Philpott, Zonke Sithole, Nomusa Sokhela, Skhumbuzo Zuma

Church Land Programme (Pietermaritzburg)
& Daraja Press (Ottawa)

Published by
Daraja Press
https://darajapress.com

&

Church Land Programme

http://churchland.org.za

Library and Archives Canada Cataloguing in Publication

Title: in, against, beyond corona : what does living through the corona crisis in South Africa reveal to us? / Mark Butler, with: Cindy Dennis, Phiwa Xulu, Zodwa Nsibande, David Ntseng, Graham Philpott, Zonke Sithole, Nomusa Sokhela, & Skhumbuzo Zuma.

Names: Butler, Mark, 1966- author.

Description: Series statement: Thinking freedom

Identifiers: Canadiana (print) 2020033364X | Canadiana (ebook) 20200333747 | ISBN 9781988832838 (softcover) | ISBN 9781988832845 (PDF)

Subjects: LCSH: COVID-19 (Disease)—Social aspects—South Africa.

Classification: LCC RA644.C67 B88 2020 | DDC 362.1962/41400968—dc23

Contents

what is padkos?

Afrikaans dictionaries translate *padkos* as 'provisions' in English. It is made up of two separate Afrikaans words: *pad,* meaning road; and *kos,* meaning food. So it describes *food for the journey*.[1]

Church Land Programme's *padkos* initiative began in 2010 as an email-list to provide and share some resources for our journey. In the beginning, those resources were limited to written pieces that come from, or connect with, the thinking and reflection that is part of our praxis. Over time, *padkos* has expanded into a vibrant and varied programme. But the core aims have remained the same, and we've always tried to ensure that the *padkos* we share is seasonal, locally-grounded, and nutritious.

WHY?

CLP has often spoken of its work as a journey, and we are inspired by Paulo Freire's phrase that "we make the path by walking". The journey of our work is deeply rewarding, and our main guide and inspiration remains the rebellious struggles of the people. But it is also a long and demanding journey. As we continue together, we all need *padkos* – sustenance and food-for-thought along the way.

CLP makes this *padkos* available because emancipatory action is always thought; because reflection strengthens struggle; and also because we have been asked to! This initiative is one aspect of our response to requests from friends & members, colleagues & comrades to be 'fed': to hear from and learn with CLP about its thinking and work.

HOW?

Padkos began as a low-traffic *email distribution list* for people directly connected with CLP, as well as fellow travelers interested in and supportive of CLP's work. In the beginning, we simply shared written pieces.

In response to the interest the readings generated, we created the *'palaver'* where we could get together to focus on a particular issue or paper, and really discuss and digest the richness and challenges. In turn, the palaver then grew into a remarkable programme of *padkos* events that draws in friends and guests, from across the country and around the world, sharing their work and thinking in interactive discussions at our offices.

We also developed a programme showing films & documentaries that has been really stimulating and enlightening. Watching them together enables us to understand, to learn from, & to make connections with other struggles in other contexts – and also with diverse modes of emancipatory organisation and struggle around the globe. We called this aspect of *padkos*, the *'bioscope'*.

Another dimension of the evolving *padkos* menu incorporated culture as a rich and nourishing part of our 'food for the journey'. *Padkos 'intermission'* has included creative events featuring, for instance, poetry & art, food & drink – and lots of live music.

Notes

1. This material first appeared in the *Padkos* series, a project of the Church Land Programme (CLP) http://churchland.org.za/.

Dawn of Darkness

Ngũgĩ wa Thiong'o

March 23, 2020[1]

I know, I know,
It threatens the common gestures of human bonding
The handshake,
The hug
The shoulders we give each other to cry on
The neighbourliness we take for granted
So much that we often beat our breasts
Crowing about rugged individualism,
Disdaining nature, pissing poison on it even, while
Claiming that property has all the legal rights of personhood
Murmuring gratitude for our shares in the gods of capital.

Oh, how now I wish I could write poetry in English,
Or any and every language you speak
So, I can share with you, words that
Wanjikũ, my Gĩkũyũ mother, used to tell me:
Gũtirĩ ũtukũ ũtakĩa:
No night is so Dark that,

It will not end in Dawn,
Or simply put,
Every night ends with dawn.
Gũtirĩ ũtukũ ũtakĩa.

This darkness too will pass away
We shall meet again and again
And talk about Darkness and Dawn
Sing and laugh maybe even hug
Nature and nurture locked in a green embrace
Celebrating every pulsation of a common being
Rediscovered and cherished for real
In the light of the Darkness and the new Dawn.

Notes

1. https://brittlepaper.com/2020/04/dawn-of-darkness-by-ngugi-wa-thiongo-poetry/

in, against, beyond corona

Introduction

What does living through the corona crisis in South Africa reveal to us? That is the question that frames our thoughts here. We've been developing this as a kind of 'document-in-progress' as our organisation[1] carefully thinks through this time of COVID-19. We had some time to discuss important elements of this material together in Zoom reflections, in addition to writing, sharing, reading and commenting. But perhaps even in its 'final' form, it will still be more a provocation for deeper reflection and debate.

Reflecting on what is revealed to us, it's important to see what is revealed as wrong and toxic – in ourselves, in our relations with others, and in our relations with the rest of non-human nature. But it's also terribly important to listen for and to seek out what is revealed that is good and life-affirming. Both are vital. During the period we were developing this reflection, we were most likely only at the beginning of the catastrophe that is/was coming according to the most influential models predicting the course of the pandemic. So, we need to sustain ourselves through what is coming, and to recognise, expand and nurture all the good things for a future where we're working together, refusing to re-create what was wrong and toxic before.

One starting point for the reflections recorded here was a conversation about whether there might be value in thinking about the Corona crisis through the lens of John Holloway's "in, against & beyond" arguments. Within our organisation, Holloway's thinking has been a central focus of our own reflections over the past years. In what follows, there may be echoes of this initial impetus but it is definitely not a systematic or exclusive 'application' of that political frame—the process took its own direction which may not have anything to do with that imagined starting point. We can't imagine that Holloway himself would be impressed by some sort of mechanical or dogmatic 'application' of his thought anyway!

Although the Corona crisis is in continuity with much that pre-existed it and that has characterised our capitalist, racist, (neo)colonial, (neo)liberal, eco-suicidal society for a long time, and although what it reveals starkly are, similarly, features that have long been present in contemporary society, nonetheless we must remain open to learning and thinking about the newness of Corona too. We would be guilty of a real laziness of thought if we simply used the crisis as an opportunity to repeat what we've been saying all along, or to validate prior analyses and programmes of action without taking on board any new learnings. Aspects of its newness and of its potential scale-of-impacts mean that for some of us this has been a moment to pause before repeating old dogmas, critiques and assertions and before leaping to un- or superficially-thought action. What we possibly confront at this time includes not only intensified rates of suffering and death, but greatly heightened levels of psycho-social anxiety and trauma. As such, this situation may call for a sense of being and presence, and not—or not only – doing and action. In reaction to flurried calls to act/do/organise/speak[2], many of the most useful responses have paused and reflected even whilst knowing also that acting/doing/organising/speaking is of course vital for our life, now and always.

And while it remains terribly important to sustain our critical vigilance at a time when powerful interests will use the crisis to leverage changes and reforms that suit them, a rigid adherence to singular explanations and reductionist analyses based on pre-existing left-critiques will not serve the present moment well either. It is clear to some of us that *this* crisis may signal the need to revisit again any possible traditional left prioritisation of the social over the individual – but without degenerating into a liberal or libertarian fetish of the individual. It is clear both need to be taken seriously – with real sensitivity to the multiplicity of different needs within all realms. Similarly, the ways in which the Corona crisis has emphatically fore-grounded the fundamentally deep sense of the interconnectedness of all people, and of all people with the rest of the environment we're in, will validate for many a sense that any worthy understanding of moving beyond this point to something radically transformed will include reference to the 'spiritual' dimension of our being and our being-together.

Perhaps we have another opportunity to re-think 'activism' too, and to recognise that for some people, a meaningful 'role' is much more one of being rather than acting. Indeed, there have been times in crisis when it becomes clear that this invisible work can be the deepest resource for others to draw on in life, and perhaps especially when normal or taken-for-granted resources that people draw on are under stress or removed. Let us also acknowledge that non-action can sometimes be a result of being overwhelmed by, or simply not clear in, a situation (like now in a time of global crisis and unimaginable loss and death)—and that that's okay. In all though, let us at least recognise that doing is indeed vital but *only* where it is thought—and that, right now, means deep and serious reflective thought.

inter-connectedness of life and lives

A global viral pandemic emphatically foregrounds inter-connectedness. Our thinking and doing in this time marks an important opportunity to learn and practise a deep understanding of that connection between all—between all people, and between people and the rest of the non-human world. It is an opportunity to see clearly the features of our current situation that are being revealed to us. It is a chance, in fact, to reclaim our doing and our relating from the morbid logics that brought us to this point of crisis, and a chance to re-orient them around other life-affirming logics. The essential character of the pandemic reveals how the system has woven our individual and collective lives together across the globe, in ways that are obviously harmful to us all, to the world, and to life itself. If we see and understand how we are made part of that deathly pattern of weaving, then we can also see that we have a choice to be, to do, and to relate, in ways that embrace and enhance life and love instead.

We apprehend that those ways of being, of doing, of relating are deeply human and are, and have always been, there in the daily rebellious refusals to conform to the world as it is, in the spaces of humanity that people defend against and beyond being stripped down to mere robots, profiteers and pen-pushers. In this way we can already look for the 'beyond' in the now.

And if there is any meaningful way to talk now about 'after' this crisis, then we should think about how we want to organise that part of human life described as 'the economy' in a way where we refuse to split it off from the totality of human life. We need to organise the economic aspects of reproducing human life according to the same values and relations that we know now to be true and nurturing for all of our humanity. Indeed, perhaps especially those values made so abundantly clear now in this crisis – of our interconnectedness, and the deep value and dignity of everything and everyone, of compassion, of kindness, of gentleness, of sensitivity and humility in our ecological relations with the world. The separation of the economic aspect from the totality of our human life and lives, allows logics other than the best of our collective humanity to be imposed. And indeed, the same goes for those aspects called 'the political'. Continuing to think that we and our creative capacities are separate from 'the economy', or indeed from 'politics', allows our current deathly pattern of 'normal' to continue on—but our refusal disrupts it.

This flows from an underlying approach that emphasises a consistent critique *ad hominem*, a critique that always reveals human agency and practice in the making of our context. So then, if the bad features emerge from our practice, and so too do the good, then it is in conscious attention to our doing (individual and collective) that we can turn away from the bad and toward the good. In that consciousness and turning, we recognise existing, as well as new, practices of everyday human and social (especially communitarian) life that defend and nurture life and its flourishing and reproduction. Here we find the real basis for going beyond in a deeply transformational and revolutionary way—the basis for a practice of doing that refuses the logic of money and power-over, for a way of doing that is intrinsically life-enhancing, emancipatory and good.

These kinds of practices can be found in a variety of arenas, and especially in traditions of resistance and rebellion—some indigenous practices as well as some practices remembered from precapitalist pasts may embody such but, equally, they can be made new in current and novel experiments and interventions. In addition, there can be few spaces of human activity not impacted by the logic of capital around the world or that do not carry their own malignancies, pathologies and oppressions from earlier periods or parallel cultures of practice/s. (So we should be wary of any claims for a pure emancipatory subject or source!)

what is revealed?

Let us take some time then, to hear and see what is being revealed about our context during or through this Corona crisis. As we've said, much of that is about the toxic aspects of our connectedness. Here we see how we are woven into (and keep re-weaving) relations and patterns-of-doing that recreate capitalism, a system which by its very nature alienates us from our selves, from our social being, and from the products of our creative doing. More than that, it establishes and accelerates rates of exploitation, harm and domination—both of people and of the 'natural' world. In fact, so many people now see that *the fundamental contradiction of our time is precisely capitalism versus life itself.* (Later, we will also take time to consider the thinking and practices that also exist 'in' our morbid and unjust situation but that counter its logic and point *beyond* it.)

So, we certainly are 'in' a situation! Corona has made some (pre-existing) features of the situation that we're in almost unbearably clear. Examples abound but we need to understand those features properly—and that also means seeing and understanding them as processes and patterns of formation emerging from our own collective practices. Certainly this crisis is helping more and more people to open their eyes and minds to think and to question what is so deeply wrong in our relations between each other and the natural world. As we noted above, this openness to thought and question is the basis for critique *ad hominem*—critique that reveals us, our relations & our activity at the centre of the reproduction of this mess.

ecology/environment

Perhaps most fundamentally, the Corona crisis makes plain this terrible contradiction: we have been made to organise ourselves for a way of reproducing *life* (defined by the logic of capitalism and domination) that is clearly and undeniably leading us to our collective, planetary *death* – and that maims and hurts us all on the way down that spiral. More and more people see now that the system that got us to this point threatens the very conditions for the possibility of reproducing human life. In this sense, Corona makes just one wave of extinction and death in a sea of our own drowning.

In our time, deadly pandemics like the one we face now, are obviously connected with the rapacious relation that our capitalist society has with the rest of the natural world that we are part of. And the evidence confirms that "humanity's 'promiscuous treatment of nature' needs to change or there will be more" such scourges:

> "Deforestation and other forms of land conversion are driving exotic species out of their evolutionary niches and into [hu]man-made environments, where they interact and breed new strains of disease, the experts say. Three-quarters of new or emerging diseases that infect humans originate in animals, according to the US Centers for Disease Control and Prevention, but it is human activity that multiplies the risks of contagion. A growing body of research confirms that bats – the origin of Covid-19 – naturally host many viruses which they are more likely transfer to humans or animals if they live in or near human-disturbed ecosystems, such as recently cleared forests or swamps drained for farmland, mining projects or residential projects. ...

> Tierra Smiley Evans, an epidemiologist at the University of California who studies virus distributions in the rapidly degrading forests of Myanmar … said the connection between environmental stress and human health had been made more apparent by Covid-19 pandemic. 'I'm hopeful that one of the most positive things to come out of horrible tragedy will be the realisation that there is a link between how we treat the forest and our wellbeing,' she said. 'It really impacts our health. It is not just a wildlife issue or an environmental issue'"[3]

Also in our country, South Africa, as well as around the world, the Corona crisis has highlighted the certain ecological deathly logic that our current capitalist 'normal' condemns us to. We have all seen the many varied and stunning instances of ecological recovery and healing being witnessed in so many places. These are flourishing simply as a result of the sudden cessation of what, till now, passed as normal economic activity, production and productivity.

Even in the city where our own organization is based, Pietermaritzburg, the air has cleared after lockdown put the brakes on economic activity. The city's principal local newspaper, *The Witness*, reported that:

> "The skies are blue, the air is clean and you can breathe much better! … Msunduzi Municipality's environmental health services, under Clive Anthony, monitors the air quality and has found that there has been a significant reduction of criteria pollutants being monitored. … Rico Euripidou, environmental

health campaigner at groundWork, said the way the air has cleaned up in some places is a remarkable testament to how unsustainable the 'normal' economy and 'normal' development is. In many places around the world, young people are seeing a clear blue sky for the first time. And millions of people with asthma are breathing easier. The benefits of the reduction in air pollution is partial and short term in SA because many of the dirtiest plants, including Eskom's big power stations, Sasol's synfuels and chemical plants, and Sapref — the country's biggest oil refinery — are still pumping out pollution. It's also short term elsewhere because governments and big corporations want the 'normal' world back again. 'The poor and most vulnerable suffer most from the health impacts of air pollution and climate change, and they will suffer most from Covid-19 and the economic crisis. That will be used to justify a return to normal, but it is precisely the normal economy that made them poor and vulnerable in the first place'."[4]

For a snapshot of the national situation, see Tony Carnie's article (8 May 2020, first published by GroundUp) based on work done by a "team of local and British scientists [which] says air pollution levels have dropped by almost half in some parts of South Africa during the six-week Covid-19 lockdown, mainly because of lower emissions from Eskom power stations and heavy industry and an absence of bumper-to-bumper traffic."[5]

As Euripidou points out above, the cessation of environmentally-damaging production that has been enforced to try to deal with the Corona virus, is a crisis in itself for capitalism. There is great pressure to re-open what has been closed as soon as possible to avoid 'catastrophe'. And it is certainly true that capitalism has made all of our lives, livelihoods and goods dependent on reproducing that system. Therefore, the results of disrupting it do indeed impact terribly on people's lives and livelihoods. But it is now surely all too clear too that the *real* catastrophe is ecological, and lies in the inevitable and accelerating spiral of death that flows from the logic of capital and of money.

inequality of life conditions and impacts

An aspect of our system that is revealed most glaringly is the material inequality of the lives we live in South Africa – and indeed, almost everywhere else too. Reflecting together as Church Land Programme, we strongly affirm that "one of the clearest revelations in this time has been to confirm just how unequal South Africa is—the size of the gaps is huge and it straddles across so many spheres of life here".

It is so grotesque that even minimum measures to contain the viral spread are simply not possible for far too many of us (for instance, washing one's hands clean regularly in soap and water, physical distancing between people, healthy eating and living for a robust immune system, ongoing access to updated information, a safe, nice domestic space within which we can lockdown and so on). Mark Heywood references a paper by Michael Sachs, a leading South African economist and former senior Treasury official, which points out that while "wealthy South Africans have seen a vast destruction of financial wealth... workers and poor communities will see the largest impact on their consumption levels".[6]

As Allen and Heese have pointed out:

> "... it is becoming clear from other countries that social and race groups are likely to experience both the virus and its repercussions differently. Emerging evidence from the US and UK – both in the eye of the storm – show that poorer communities are more likely to be adversely affected. ...
>
> In SA one's ability to practise social-distancing and

> lessen the risk of contracting Covid-19 is clearly a function of wealth and access to resources. There are a number of key areas that specifically define the challenges faced by the poor in self-isolating: living in informal housing; large household size; inadequate access to water and sanitation; reliance on public transport; high population density; and low annual income. … In SA access to healthcare likely reflects poverty and the risk of contagion can be assumed to be predominantly among those who have limited access to services, as well as those living in densely populated areas and large households". [7]

In a terribly ironic and obvious contrast, so much of middle-class suburban life – which remains a dominant collective aspirational model – is already a mode of 'socially distant' living, and the prescribed containment measures are that much easier to achieve.

urban concentration – including shack settlements

We need to reflect seriously on the fact that the viral impact is concentrated in urban areas. Many other, and related, contemporary, abiding environmental and human psychological and spiritual afflictions are similarly concentrated. Accordingly, we must ask ourselves what is the appropriate human and ecological scale and patterning for co-living and settlement if we want to achieve a convivial, healthful and sustainable future for human society? Far too many people live in overly-crowded urban settlements with distressingly too little space for connections with nature – plants, birds, insects, and the like (gardens, allotments, vegetable gardens, common green spaces, wild spaces and so on). The separation of humans from our connectedness with the rest of nature is very damaging to our whole human being.

neo-liberalism

We see clearly now the devastating impact and legacy of our (relatively recent) neo-liberal assault on, and hollowing-out of, 'the public' – both as institutional/material fact (for instance the miserably-inadequate state and extent of public health infrastructure) but also, and at least as (if not more) important, as a set of values and ideas to orient our collective and individual doing and ethics around (for instance, the naked disregard for the other in self-serving actions against distancing or for purchasing). We see clearly now neo-liberalism's devastating impact of relentlessly monetising everything we touch, of turning everything into a commodity to be sold and bought – it is destroying the conditions of life, and enveloping the globe in waves of plague and misery.

the thinking or attitude of the (South African) state

South Africans have seen how the lockdown provisions that were decreed by the state have been enforced. On balance, there has been far too little implementation based on consensus, common sense, information, popular education and respect for people's dignity and intelligence. Instead, we have seen enforcement through the significant deployment of police and army forces. This is the mode of 'masculine' muscular & militarised power-over that is the default posture of state authority over the people. To be fair, the state speaks in contradictory ways about the deployment of armed forces to enforce lockdown measures, including sometimes a gentler language that imagines this deployment of personnel as friends of the people in a time of crisis. But tragically it is clear that another way is a bullying thuggery that relishes the imposition of military control over the streets. As City Press has commented:

> "[t]he relationship between a citizenry and a country's police force is not – and should never be – adversarial. With equal weight, the relationship with the military, when deployed for civil duty, should also not be adversarial. Both these arms of protection are employed by the people they serve. ... The lockdown in South Africa ... should not come at the expense of human rights and the right to life. Reports so far reflect a dark picture of alleged abuse of citizens at the hands of their protectors. ... Some have been beaten. Some have died. This borders on Gestapo tactics and is in violation of the very nature of our constitutionally entrenched human rights."[8]

Without access to sufficient data we can't confidently extrapolate but anecdotally it does seem the latter mode of enforcement seems more prevalent in contexts where historic nationalist struggles to overthrow settler-colonial regimes were followed by regimes that inherited and parroted the tools and attitudes of colonial rule over people—especially black people.

In a particularly shameful egregious period – and against national law, lockdown regulations and Ministerial pronouncements – the City of Durban has unleashed privatised security forces against shack settlements destroying homes shack-dwellers had created.[9]

So, in a sense, we can argue that one thing that has not shifted really is the practice of government to think for people and not with them, to act for people and not with them. For instance, democratically-organised local formations in shack settlements would be an obvious and primary partner in the conversations about life in those contexts at this time of looming crisis—conversations that have never been more critical, but that are almost entirely absent. This is disastrous. It's correct to point out that the containment measures declared by government are easier and more feasible in middle- and upper-class contexts than for those millions of South Africans living in over-crowded homes and densely-populated settlements marked by deep poverty and a dearth of public infrastructures and private space and facilities. But that reality should only be the *start* of a very serious conversation about what to do there in the light of the Corona crisis. Instead of conversation though, we have varying and wildly-uneven degrees of compliance in terms of the very basic measures of containment, and mutual suspicion and mistrust, even antagonism. And when we talk of 'conversation' here, we do not mean the kind of manipulative 'consultation' that the state has invariably deployed till now when claiming to consult, engage and listen to the public. We mean a conversation based on a mutual recognition of the dignity and capacity for intelligence and learning of all—including the state. It is striking how relatively few resources have been directed to deploying trained and informed people and learning-materials for popular education and mutual learning about what this Corona crisis is and what we all have to do in the face of it, compared to resource allocations for the military deployment and business support for instance. As the more draconian lockdown features have been progressively eased, there has been less space for aggressive enforcement of curfews, restrictions of people's movements and the like. But the opportunities for significant and credible information sharing between the state and the people have largely been squandered – and the state's armed wings have shown themselves to be remarkably inept at safeguarding freedom and dignity, or fostering a culture of caring and kindness – let alone understanding and defending a nominally-democratic constitutional order!

There's an important area of discussion that's emerged through our reflections together about how to read the response of the state. There's consensus that, in the current situation, the logic of capital dominates in the end. In a sense, this is not surprising—we're a capitalist society with a capitalist state in a (predominantly neo-liberal) capitalist world. For some of us, everything the state has done in response to the Corona virus reflects this logic, and shows that leaders and politicians make choices consciously to favour the rich and the capitalists, and to exploit, marginalise and attack the poor and the working class. But we've had discussions about how important it is to pay attention to the moments and ways in which this crisis has forced the state to take on board a logic that disrupts that of neo-liberal capitalism, of money and profit, and to insert the logic of our common and shared humanity instead. Some of us have suggested that we trap ourselves into a kind of self-fulfilling left-fatalism if we ignore these disruptions to the logic of money by a countervailing logic of our common and connected humanity. There are strong indications that, unless enough of us rebel and refuse, the neo-liberals[10] will push hard and reimpose that logic onto our 'post-COVID' trajectories—but it is not enough to be able say "we told you so" *as if no other possibility exists.*

domestic life, psychological stress

At a global level, WHO's mental health department director, Devora Kestel warned of another looming crisis: "The isolation, the fear, the uncertainty, the economic turmoil—they all cause or could cause psychological distress". According the *Guardian*:

> "she said the world could expect to see an upsurge in the severity of mental illness, including amongst children, young people and healthcare workers. 'The mental health and wellbeing of whole societies have been severely impacted by this crisis and are a priority to be addressed urgently.'[11]

Also in Mid-May, the results of a major South African survey were reported on by Mark Orkin and others[12]. The large-scale Covid-19 democracy survey was conducted jointly by the University of Johannesburg's Centre for Social Change and the Developmental, Capable and Ethical State research division of the Human Sciences Research Council. It found that 33% of South African adults were depressed, 45% fearful, and 29% lonely during lockdown. An April 2020 academic article warns that "It appears likely that there will be substantial increases in anxiety and depression, substance use, loneliness, and domestic violence."

Orkin *et al* state:

> "We may illustrate ... with poignant answers to our invitation to survey respondents to share, in their own words, "the worst thing" about lockdown:
>
> **Scared:** "There is no limit to the people coming into the store. So it put me and my colleagues at high risk to get infected."
>
> **Stressed:** "Knowing that my parents are stressed about where we are going to get our next meal if the President decides to extend the lockdown."
>
> **Depressed:** "The lockdown has affected my business harshly, production has stopped all together. At times I feel depressed, feel like life is not worth living anymore."
>
> **Sad:** "Watching my kids get sad and angry at the restrictions and I cannot take them outside."
>
> **Irritable:** "No take-aways, no liquor stores or cigarette sales. Getting frustrated with my household and enormous pressure due to school children missing a lot of work."
>
> **Angry:** "Being locked even when I feel like both going somewhere I want to—it makes me angry so much."
>
> **Bored:** "Not being able to go to school or not seeing my

> friends. Also it gets boring cause we don't have WiFi or data."
>
> **Lonely:** "I cannot really help my elderly mom and she is very lonely."
>
> ... Adding in another statistical technique, called regression analysis, we are able to tackle a key issue: among the range of topics covered in the survey, what are the chief drivers of these phenomena, so that their components may be mitigated? It turns out that much the strongest predictor of composite psychological distress is sheer hunger. This is, tragically, no surprise. ... In response to the "worst thing" write-in option, the most frequent response, 31%, was not having enough food to eat: "I am an unemployed mother of three kids and I don't know where my next meal is coming from"; "I am living with a granny and hunger is killing us"; "Hunger and the fear of dying out of hunger since no income".

The lockdown provisions exposed the horror that, for so many people, our intimate spaces of domestic, personal and relational life are powder kegs of simmering violence, frustration and dehumanisation. Writing in late-April about the lockdown, Mark Heywood noted that "the social toll on the poor is now manifest; the most visible sign is in hunger and hunger 'riots'. But unmeasured and below the radar line are tectonic levels of anxiety, fear, stress and probably interpersonal violence."[13]

Movements of the poor and oppressed often reflect on how the truth of their lives and struggles remain 'unmeasured and below the radar line' of what is counted in society – and women's truth all too frequently remains more deeply hidden even. The Women's League of the South African shack-dweller movement, Abahlali baseMjondolo, have said that under conditions of Corona-lockdown, "[w]e are subject to constant abuse by the government and men in our own communities. ... We as women living in shacks are suffering because of the way we live with families of children and a father in one room. ... We are also robbed and raped in our houses. ... We are plagued by worrying about the men who are killing us, beating us and sexually abusing us and our children. ... It seems like we are on our own as women. If we don't support each other we will perish. Building women's power in struggle is the only way forward ... to ensure that women are respected as equals everywhere, in homes, communities, workplaces and on the streets."[14]

Indeed, it may well be high time to seriously re-think our (historically largely capitalist and western) assumption that the isolated nuclear family should be the default basis for organising domestic space and life. As Suzanne Moore has commented for instance: "extended families or more communal ways of living are better at caring for children and elderly people. Instead, we consign care to low paid people who are little valued. Loneliness was a societal problem long before Corona."[15]

Consequences of the Corona crisis, as well its related lockdown measures, have undoubtedly resulted in enormous socio-psychological stresses that many people are enduring. Awareness, support, resources and appropriate actions are very un-even in response, but this is a huge and important area requiring attention. Some people came into this period of crisis already more predisposed to psychological stress and need special concern and support. Now, many more are also stressed by factors directly associated with the virus and its preventative measures—for instance, livelihood and income scarcity and uncertainty; or interpersonal tensions from being confined together with others in small spaces for long periods; or isolation and disconnection from healthy social interactions that are being disrupted by rules to achieve distancing; or pervasive and generalised underlying sense of loss, grief, trauma and mourning in the awareness of suffering and death caused by the pandemic. All these point to the light and the shadow of our fundamental connectedness across humanity and the world. Some of it will progressively lift as the pandemic recedes and the restrictions can be increasingly relaxed. But some will remain. And some of our awareness, and the caring and nurturing that should flow from it, should certainly remain with us as we move 'beyond'.

Indeed for some, where the domestic conditions of lockdown are not intolerable, there have been new positive opportunities to, for example, become more aware of and involved in the otherwise hidden labours of domestic life. People who are currently prevented from leaving the home to go out to work (as may have been their daily practice up till now), have had a chance to connect more with tasks like child-care and interaction, or food preparation and household cleaning. While for some this has been a pain in the ass, there is a positive possibility for the future to value and share more equitably the work of human connection, caring and reproducing life. Later, when we consider ways that are indicated for going 'beyond' what is and has been, we should recall and expand this insight to re-imagine and re-practice how to reproduce abundant and healthy and fulfilling human life, including in the 'small' spaces of immediate relations and domesticity.

We must also acknowledge that, in the face of these stresses and the massive uncertainty this crisis has heralded, many people grab onto conspiracy theories and wildly fantastical 'explanations'. As Melanie Verwoerd has noted:

> "As human beings we don't like uncertainty or feeling out of control. We like to know that someone has a plan or that we can make our own plans. Otherwise, life feels just too unpredictable and dangerous. It is therefore not surprising that there is such a tsunami of conspiracy theories at the moment. The narrative of conspiracy theories are

all the same. 'A big evil person or persons hatching out an evil plan to control us (the masses) so that they can benefit while we suffer.' ... Even though these conspiracy theories are often laughable, they still provide people with a sense of certainty. ... And so they give people a (false) sense of control".[16]

[dis]connections and [un]commons

In a country like ours, the stress that the Corona crisis is placing on society can tell us something about the abiding, but also complex, ways in which our making of race and racism continues to structure our collective / shared life. It is certainly true that deep poverty and material distress continues to be mostly a black experience, and that whiteness more often than blackness correlates with privilege. But it's also true that (a) we make and re-make race and the practices of racism, and (b) a quarter of a century after the end of the apartheid state, there are important exceptions and deviations from any crude mapping of these issues[17]. For ourselves as a society, it is important to be honest, and it is dangerous not to recognise that a crisis of the current portent really does ultimately implicate all, even if difference and inequality must also be recognised and held in critical tension.

Measures to contain and respond to the Corona crisis really only work when they are taken up as shared responsibilities by all, and for all. But our society is deeply unequal and uneven, and compliance has proven deeply unequal and uneven too. We have noted how distressing it is to see that the kind of order imposed by the state via the police and the military reveals the state's violent and abusive face over the people. On the other hand, many are also dismayed at the sometimes staggering displays of contempt for the measures to contain and respond to the Corona crisis, and for the logic of collective humanity and shared crisis and responsibility that informs their necessity. In the current situation, those measures that our society as a whole requires, calls on each of us to act in solidarity for the greater good.

The actions of those pockets of people[18] demonstrating varying degrees of disregard for the measures put in place for the greater good, demonstrate a distressing lack of concern for that greater good, of any real sense of connection with the broader community of humanity. Furthermore, their actions sometimes seem to be predicated on an assumed impunity for acting recklessly in self-interest. In a way this is simply one part of the value-set of the Zuma-era writ large (and hardly unique to South Africa by the way—witness identical patterns in spaces around the globe where populist hucksters have gained popular traction). But each place's version of its history and its current moment offers up the materials for constructing (false and dangerous) justificatory narratives they believe justifies their exceptionalism – their belief that the rules either don't apply to them or are being imposed on them because of some fundamental unfairness or evil. These narratives of exceptionalism routinely tell of perpetual victimhood at the hands of variously constructed 'others'. These 'others' are then routinely cast or imagined as enjoying some idyllic life of mastery and untrammeled power, unrestrained consumption and freedom, while conspiring to deny their servile victims that imagined idyllic life of untrammeled personal or communal power, unrestrained consumption and 'freedom'. To call for moderation, restraint, curtailed activity and sobriety is to risk being cast as that 'other', or its pathetic and manipulated puppet. This tendency aligns itself in a very unhealthy combination with that mentioned already above in terms of people's attraction to conspiracy theories in times of uncertainty and stress.

These truths are uncomfortable and, as noted above, need always to be held together (if in tension) with knowing the truth of our unequal society. As an anonymous [middle-class] contributor to the *Daily Maverick* paper has pointed out, we need to

> "think about the situation the vast majority of our people find themselves in. It is not possible to self-isolate in an overcrowded house or in a shack. There is no WiFi or internet to entertain and alleviate the boredom. The only place, in those conditions, to remain sane, is on the street outside. And now, after three weeks of not being allowed to go to work, those who once had jobs no longer have money to buy food and they join those who never had food in the first place. What are people meant to do? What can I do to show my solidarity? How can I concretise the notion that we are all in this together. Be aware that people who can barely afford not to go to work have been forced into the lockdown so that all of us, collectively, can be safe."[19]

To some extent, disregard for lockdown-type containment measures may also reflect a much broader lack of moral legitimacy and authority of the state in the eyes of many people. If so, it is the state's consistent lack of trust in, and respect for, the people that inaugurated the cycle.

what points beyond?

It is irrefutably clear that many of the good things we've seen in this time of crisis and death are really good but they are absolutely incompatible with capitalism—things like the dramatic brake on consumerism; radically cutting pollution; more time thinking and caring than 'working'; prioritising and allocating material, intellectual, social, infrastructural resources precisely against the logic of money and market demand and instead to the poor, the public, the vulnerable, the carers, and so on.

Logically, we conclude then that what is centrally revealed about our situation—and perhaps revealed anew to people who had perhaps forgotten its abiding truth—is the spectacular inappropriateness of the logic of money/capital to human (humane and social) life. We've seen how the Corona crisis highlights the disastrous impact of this logic when it shapes the organisation of our relations between people, and also between humans and non-human nature.

It is clearer than ever, that we need a completely different ecological relation to the world we're in—not dominating but fraternal; not exploitative but regenerative; not mercenary but reciprocal; not competitive but communist; not promiscuous but nurturing; not aggressive and hurtful but mutually healing and restorative.

But without our stubborn and militant refusal, the logic of money will reimpose itself and we will return to literal 'business' as usual. And it is now surely clear and urgent to see that what has passed for normality, is a "normality of death" (a phrase used by John Holloway in an interview with Firoze Manji of Daraja Press.)[20] Clearly, an important battle ahead will be the contestation over how we 'start again', over what vision, practices, relations and principles will shape what comes next.

As Steven Friedman says,[21] "just about everyone agrees the pandemic will change the world forever. Just about no-one agrees on what the new world will be or should be". He points out how people are arguing that, because the pandemic has exposed the environmental devastation and social inequality that marked our "normal", we can avoid them in a post-pandemic future. Of course it's true we can (and indeed we should), and it's true that "the pandemic may trigger these changes. But it might equally usher in the polar opposite" and also possible that "the new world will not be that new after all". Friedman argues:

> "None of these routes will emerge automatically ... [I]t will depend on whether those who want a fairer, more democratic world, better able to save the planet, are stronger and make better strategic decisions than those who want the opposite. [But] those who want a fairer world have it in their power to defeat the merchants of hate and *dictatorship"*.[22]

A lot of the contestation over what comes next relates to questions of the economy. Indeed, there's a lot of talk about the economy. Some of it focuses on the economic challenges to come after the peak of the Corona crisis period. Some of it considers economic questions arising during the crisis management period itself. Some of that talk is driven by the interests of capital (and fractions within capital)—and within that are clearly opportunistic interventions to try to push through unpalatable structural reforms at the height of a crisis. These voices are powerful – and current minister on finance, Tito Mboweni, is likely quite attentive to them given his neo-liberal tendency. But many other South Africans also focus on questions of the economy and how the virus and its counter measures[23] are already, and will, negatively impact, with disastrous consequences for the poor not just big (and other) business. During the period of national 'management' of the crisis, there is urgent need for wide and meaningful direction of social measures and material resources to the poor[24].

We've said we want to pay attention to what the Corona crisis reveals to us about the situation we are in. We've also said it reveals connectedness, and that that connectedness has both toxic and benign aspects. Thus far, we have mostly considered some dimensions of the toxicity of our situation. We have seen how our current situation is deeply structured by capitalism and as such has made all of our lives, livelihoods, relations and goods tied up with, and dependent on, reproducing that system. But it is now surely also clear that the real catastrophe is the inevitable and accelerating spiral of death that flows from that logic of capital and of money.

The positive is that we can take hold of this insight and hope that it, together with new (and old too) forms of experimenting in radically different ways of doing/being/relating that flow from it, can be sustained beyond the immediate Corona crisis. In fact, is this not a really important aspect for us all to work on now? – encouraging people to identify these areas and think/act them as a present future, planning and imagining how to extend them forward in time, and expand them to growing spheres of life.

And we do wonder whether kindness, social solidarity, and an appropriate scale of time, aren't perhaps the most important of these? During a collective reflection between colleagues, a widely held insight was that "for many of us, the lockdown had the unexpected and liberating effect of opening or halting time – of allowing us to stop and reflect in a way that wasn't there before under the kind of time-regime dictated by the business-as-usual before lockdown. In this novel sense of time, we became newly aware of how precious life is, and how precious our connection with others and the world is—we should never take these for granted again".

And this is why we must orient ourselves in the real present to finding and celebrating the good, to noting and nurturing the thinking and doing that rejects the logic of power-over, of competition or profit, of exploitation and humiliation. This is not only to sustain hope and balance pessimism – though perhaps there's no harm in recognising that's part of its function. Much more fundamentally, it's absolutely imperative if we are serious about changing the world! We know by now the futility of old left-traditions of thought and practice that assume change will come from tiny vanguard groups of activists whose thinking is somehow 'advanced', and needs to be conveyed to the masses in order to achieve revolutionary change. We are much more likely to actually change the world when we listen and tap into all the many ways in which people's own questions and thinking, their ways of relating and acting, refuse the logic of toxic power and monetised exchange for profit. Here, we will discover already-existing breaks with that logic of money and power. Here we encounter practices that, instead, embody and embrace the values and principles for a better way of reproducing life. This almost certainly requires looking beyond old-style leftist sects and dogmas as we seek out and grow the non-toxic and the life-affirming that exists already in the 'thoughts, words and deeds' of many people and groups.

Now as ever, it is our thinking and our doing that will either re-create what went before or expand the spaces where we refuse that and 'walk in a different direction' instead (drawing on some of John Holloway's language).

So if we consider the situation of the masses of urban poor discussed earlier for instance, our actions now and going forward must not (simply) recreate the conditions of life that we now list as reasons why, for instance, precautionary measures to contain viral spread and take care of ourselves are not possible for so many people[25]. Thus for example, it is clear that we *all* know now that all human settlements need humane dimensions of space – inside and out, personal, domestic and communal; we know that *all* people need good and sufficient food (local organic production that people are connected with and so on); and that *all* people need primary, holistic, immune-boosting and preventative health, and clean air and water, that *all* people need access to mutual, open, reliable and honest information and communication; and also to care (and to widely-practiced caring attitudes) for everyone, especially to those battling psychologically or with issues like addiction and so on.

In the same way, we must state the unavoidable and deeper implications of what has been revealed so that we stop re-creating, through our actions and attitudes, all the social and psycho-social malignancies that we have shown to be highlighted and exacerbated under lockdown—here we are recalling aspects like domestic violence and tyranny, but also deeper spiritual malaises of capitalist modernity like finding real human meaning, contentment, connection and value disconnected from (capitalist-defined) productivity and consumption. By expanding the spaces of life where we refuse to continue hurtful practices, we undo a broader web that has trapped us into patterns of death.

Perhaps a task for all of us then is to try to list all the good and heartening things we're witnessing now. What could our criteria be for putting things on this list? Perhaps a combination of certain values that seem vital now (or at least whose vitality for all life/time has become clearer right now perhaps), together with a more or less clear break (either now, deliberately or by 'chance', or have always broken) with the logic of money/capital/domination/hurt. Those values would include: kindness, caring, neighbourliness, solidarity, conviviality, generosity, affirmation and encouragement, heartwarming, nurturing, modest, simplicity... what else would you add?

Notes

1. The Church Land Programme (CLP)
2. An illustration of a left rush to act, that re-inscribes the architecture of oppression and silencing? Early on in the pandemic, a metropolitan-centred group of professional vanguardist activists got together via on-line modalities to draft a *people*'s charter for the COVID crisis!
3. Jonathan Watts, 7 May 2020. "Promiscuous treatment of nature will lead to more pandemics - scientists" *The Guardian,* https://www.theguardian.com/environment/2020/may/07/promiscuous-treatment-of-nature-will-lead-to-more-pandemics-scientists.

4. Sharika Regchand, 20 April 2020, *"City enjoys cleaner air"* https://m.news24.com/SouthAfrica/News/city-enjoys-cleaner-air-20200420-2.

5. https://www.dailymaverick.co.za/article/2020-05-08-enjoy-the-fresh-air-while-it-lasts-lockdown-banishes-air-pollution/

6. Mark Heywood, 20 April 2020. *A Time of Reckoning"* https://www.dailymaverick.co.za/article/2020-04-20-a-time-of-reckoning/

7. Kevin Allan and Karen Heese, 10 April 2020. Covid-19 affects the poor more than others, and even more so in SA. https://www.businesslive.co.za/bd/opinion/2020-04-10-covid-19-affects-the-poor-more-than-others-and-even-more-so-in-sa/.

8. City Press Editorial, 19 April 2020. "Bheki Cele, we are neither a police nor a military state."https://city-press.news24.com/Voices/editorial-bheki-cele-we-are-neither-a-police-nor-a-military-state-20200419.

9. For a fuller examination of, and response to, this outrage, see CLP's independent research report: *"Stop Illegal Evictions"*, 2020.

10. We should also note that within the ruling party and government, there appears to be something of an ongoing—or even re-vitalised - contestation between those more ideologically aligned to neo-liberalism and those who would favour a return to the language and practice of the 'developmental [capitalist] state'. For the latter grouping, the Corona period has re-awakened a feeling (almost nostalgic by now after years of neo-liberal assault) for the 'strong' state, imposing direction on the people and the economy from a centralised 'command centre' and so on.

11. https://www.theguardian.com/world/2020/may/14/global-report-who-says-covid-19-may-never-go-and-warns-of-mental-health-crisis

12. See: "The hidden struggle: The mental health effects of the Covid-19 lockdown in South Africa", Mark Orkin, Benjamin Roberts, Narnia Bohler-Muller & Kate Alexander, 13 May 2020, *Daily Maverick*, https://www.dailymaverick.co.za/article/2020-05-13-the-hidden-struggle-the-mental-health-effects-of-the-covid-19-lockdownin-south-africa/

13. Mark Heywood, 20 April 2020. *"A Time of Reckoning"* https://www.dailymaverick.co.za/article/2020-04-20-a-time-of-reckoning/

14. Abahlali baseMjondolo Women's League, June 2020. "The Lives of Women & Girls Are Not Respected", 8 June 2020, Abahlali baseMjondolo Women's League Press Statement.

15. Suzanne Moore, 20 April 2020, in a comment to readers written after publication of her article: "The way we once lived is now redundant we need to reinvent ourselves" https://www.theguardian.com/world/commentisfree/2020/apr/20/the-way-we-once-lived-is-now-redundant-we-need-to-reinvent-ourselves

16. "Are the conspiracy theories true?", 8 May 2020. https://m.news24.com/Columnists/MelanieVerwoerd/melanie-verwoerd-are-the-conspiracy-theories-true-20200508-2

17. Thus for instance, it is simply and empirically not true that *all* poor, homeless, negatively-effected economic projects, and so on are black, and equally, not *all* who have been able to sustain their capacity to enjoy space, mobility, information and internet access, and decent nutrition are white.

18. And to be clear, these would include instances and practices of selfish recklessness and communal frivolity across all social sectors.

19. Anonymous. "Ask yourself: What can I do?" *Daily Maverick* 21 April 2020. https://www.dailymaverick.co.za/article/2020-04-21-ask-yourself-what-can-i-do/

20. https://darajapress.com/2020/06/17/john-holloway-a-cascade-of-angers-my-covid-19-fantasy, June 2020

21. 14 April 2020, "Tackling inequality and helping the poor a priority in post-pandemic world" https://www.businesslive.co.za/bd/opinion/columnists/2020-04-14-steven-friedman-tackling-inequality-and-helping-the-poor-a-priority-in-post-pandemic-world/

22. ibid.

23. For instance, during May the national lockdown was estimated to be causing an estimated R13-billion per day loss to GDP. Quoted in Mark Heywood, 20 April 2020. "A Time of Reckoning", Daily Maverick. https://www.dailymaverick.co.za/article/2020-04-20-a-time-of-reckoning/

24. See for instance: Mark Heywood, 20 April 2020. "A Time of Reckoning" https://www.dailymaverick.co.za/article/2020-04-20-a-time-of-reckoning/)

25. This is not to say that everyone deserves a life of isolation (on the contrary!) and nor that everyone should aspire to anything more than a simple, modest and good life with the mutual recognition of

dignities at its heart.

Lockdown

Brother Richard Hendrick

March 13th, 2020

Yes there is fear.
Yes there is isolation.
Yes there is panic buying.
Yes there is sickness.
Yes there is even death.
But,
They say that in Wuhan after so many years of noise
You can hear the birds again.
They say that after just a few weeks of quiet
The sky is no longer thick with fumes
But blue and grey and clear.
They say that in the streets of Assisi
People are singing to each other
across the empty squares,
keeping their windows open
so that those who are alone
may hear the sounds of family around them.
They say that a hotel in the West of Ireland

Is offering free meals and delivery to the housebound.
Today a young woman I know
is busy spreading fliers with her number
through the neighbourhood
So that the elders may have someone to call on.
Today Churches, Synagogues, Mosques and Temples
are preparing to welcome
and shelter the homeless, the sick, the weary
All over the world people are slowing down and reflecting
All over the world people are looking at their neighbours in a new way
All over the world people are waking up to a new reality
To how big we really are.
To how little control we really have.
To what really matters.
To Love.
So we pray and we remember that
Yes there is fear.
But there does not have to be hate.
Yes there is isolation.
But there does not have to be loneliness.
Yes there is panic buying.
But there does not have to be meanness.
Yes there is sickness.
But there does not have to be disease of the soul
Yes there is even death.
But there can always be a rebirth of love.
Wake to the choices you make as to how to live now.
Today, breathe.
Listen, behind the factory noises of your panic
The birds are singing again
The sky is clearing,
Spring is coming,

And we are always encompassed by Love.
Open the windows of your soul
And though you may not be able
to touch across the empty square,
Sing.

A sustainable place where even the poorest can prosper

In our paper *in, against, beyond corona,* we said "it's important to see what is revealed to be wrong and toxic—in ourselves, in our relations with others, and in our relation with the rest of non-human nature. But it's also terribly important to listen for and to seek out what is revealed that is good and life-affirming. Both are vital". Subsequently in our *padkos* series, we also shared Nomfundo Xolo's account of collective food production at the shack settlement of eKhenana, in our neighbouring city of eThekwini, that was recently published by *New Frame.*

The people of eKhenana were central to our recent Church Land Programme research report on brutal waves of attacks and evictions targeting shack settlements in the city of eThekwini/ Durban.[1] Little has been more toxic during this period than the inhumanity and violence of this campaign of violence waged against poor people. And yet, not only do the people remain, and not only do they defend and rebuild, they are also engaged in a programme of collective thought and of food production. Xolo's article for *New Frame* captures important elements of this remarkable, and ultimately inspiring, mix of courage, tenacity, thought and and action, for life and autonomy against death. You'll read about a collective community-based food production initiative that has unfolded alongside self-run political classes – and relentless defense and re-building of the settlement itself against state harassment and violence.

A resident, 26 year old Samkelo Majiya, says "We arrived here when it was just a dense, neglected forest. ... When we got together, we identified this place and gradually claimed it as our new home because we were discarded by the ... system". Ayanda Mjila, says "We are not land invaders or illegal occupants. We are committed to creating a sustainable place where even the poorest can prosper". An elected leader in the settlement, Lindokuhle Mnguni, is quoted saying: "As young people with historical poverty attached to our names, we need to start promoting the concept of developing practical pathways that ... challenge the ... corporate-controlled food system based on capitalism and tackle food inequality at its roots".

These developments are really significant. Discussing the meaning of food sovereignty for our own work and context a number of years ago, CLP argued that "if food sovereignty in South Africa is to be truly rooted, and remain faithful to its origins, then it can only emerge in and through the self-defined and self-led struggles of real people – especially the landless and peasant farmers. Genuine movements of the landless and the rural poor are certainly not dead but we must be honest and recognise they are weak. One result is that activists, NGOs and vanguardists of 'civil society' relentlessly step in and try to manufacture food sovereignty. This is impossible. It merely replicates the patterns of abuse, contempt and 'representation' that were at the heart of food sovereignty at the beginning".

eKhenana residents are tilling for freedom

Nomfundo Xolo
13 Aug 2020

The following article was first published by New Frame. https://www.newframe.com/ekhenana-residents-are-tilling-for-freedom/

Residents of eKhenana, a land occupation in Cato Manor, Durban, have started planting vegetables. Food sovereignty and other forms of self-sufficiency, they say, will be achieved through tilling the soil and opening themselves up to new knowledge.

The settlement was created in 2018. Many of its residents came from rented lodgings in a nearby area. After facing evictions, they decided to establish a new community. They named it eKhenana, isiZulu for Canaan. Residents say the name represents their aspirations. They want to transform eKhenana into a place fit for humans, with all the residents' needs catered for.

"As young people with historical poverty attached to our names, we need to start promoting the concept of developing practical pathways that ... challenge the ... corporate-controlled food system based on capitalism and tackle food inequality at its roots," says Lindokuhle Mnguni, the elected leader of the eKhenana settlement. "This will enable many South Africans who are affected by poverty with limited access to information and healthy choices to develop customised alternatives that could change our relationship with food sovereignty and sustainability."

There are 109 families on two hectares of land, one of which is dedicated to farming. Each family has a small plot on which a shack is built with recycled materials.

Mnguni says their community was inspired by Brazil's Landless Workers Movement (*Movimento dos Trabalhadores Rurais Sem*

Terra or MST), which is based on Marxist and liberation ideologies. MST emphases equality and the transformation of capitalist society through agriculture, cooperation and the protection of the environment. To apply these ideas, the community gets help from the shack dwellers' movement Abahlali baseMjondolo, to which it is affiliated as a branch.

It is not enough to only work the land. Community members must know why it is important to be self-sufficient. Mguni and his team have developed educational programmes covering the importance of food sovereignty, among other concerns.

'We are not land invaders'

"We arrived here when it was just a dense, neglected forest," says Samkelo Majiya, 26, a resident of eKhenana. "We all had been experiencing similar challenges of eviction and unemployment. When we got together, we identified this place and gradually claimed it as our new home because we were discarded by the same system that is expected to prioritise the poor South Africans who suffer historical oppression. Our parents have passed on waiting. We cannot watch as more generational poverty continues to widen in South Africa."

eKhenana is an offshoot of Cato Manor, one of the oldest shack settlements in Durban and home to about 90 000 people. Many settled in the area because of its proximity to the city.

Ayanda Mjila, 28, talks about the group's historical struggles. He says that each week they hold classes to share information on political education, English as a communication tool and strategies for the survival of the food projects.

"The life we are trying to adopt in eKhenana allows for an opportunity to discuss how land and the debate on land expropriation can be used in the urban context, to ensure that unused unproductive vacant land in cities can be expropriated for the provision of housing and other services for the urban poor.

"We are not land invaders or illegal occupants. We are committed to creating a sustainable place where even the poorest can prosper. We have made efforts to try mitigate the socioeconomic problems brought about by apartheid, and the consequence of a corrupt system meant to liberate us 26 years ago," says Mjila.

Covid-19 and evictions

Many eKhenana residents are young adults, some with families, and each with complex, disparate backgrounds. But they all fear being evicted. Settlements similar to theirs, and nearby, have been razed to the ground.

Covid-19 has not helped. Many in the community have lost jobs because of the hard lockdown. Statistics South Africa revealed that unemployment figures have risen sharply in recent months.

A research report by the Church Land Programme into the eviction of shack dwellers in eThekwini during the early days of the hard lockdown showed that there has been a total of 18 illegal evictions in eKhenana, Azania and Ekuphumeleleni settlements. About 900 people were affected.

"On 21 and 22 April, Calvin and Family Security violently attacked the eKhenana settlement in Cato Crest by firing live ammunition at unarmed people, destroying homes, stealing possessions as well as subjecting residents to abuse. This is following an interdict that the 109 families in eKhenana successfully secured ... from the Durban high court against the illegal evictions occurring," reads the report.

"We are South African residents who are victims of otherwise avoidable circumstances," says Nokuthula Mabaso, 37. "We are born into poverty, but we are expected to progress into an unattainable lifestyle. The current South African system does not seem to favour the poor citizens. We are left to fend for ourselves, but what is a man's wealth when he has no land? And how is a native man homeless after our forefathers and fathers fought for equal rights and justice for all?"

Tired of rebuilding

Since its establishment, eKhenana has been under siege from the eThekwini Municipality, residents say. They have had to rebuild their homes many times over.

Recently, the settlement experienced another eviction. Abahlali baseMjondolo released a statement condemning the incident: "On 28 July 2020, the occupation was attacked by the Metro Police, the anti-land invasion unit and Calvin and Family Security. They destroyed 13 homes and stole the building materials. They also stole people's personal property, money and lots of cellphones. Two people were seriously injured in the attack and are now in King Edward Hospital.

"The residents of this occupation are protected by a court order that was granted on 27 December 2019, and then reaffirmed on 24 April 2020 after the municipality repeatedly attacked the settlement in violation of the court order, the Constitution, the law and the lockdown regulations,"

Phumelele Mkhize, 29, was beaten with the back of guns carried by the attackers and cut on the arm with a bush knife while sitting inside her home. Msawakhe Magwaza, 30, was also hit with the back of guns. Kwanele Mhlongo, a 15-year-old with learning difficulties, was severely beaten. Mnguni, the settlement's leader, was also injured.

Despite the threat of mass evictions and violence, residents continue to till the soil and plant seeds, looking forward to food sovereignty in the promised land.

Notes

1. see *Padkos* no: 99: STOP Corona Evictions! [http://www.church-land.org.za/?page_id=3734] and, for the report itself: http://www.churchland.org.za/wp-content/uploads/2020/06/STOP-Illegal-evictions.pdf

What cities can learn from lockdown about planning for life after the Coronavirus pandemic

Jill L Grant

28 April 2020

This article first appeared in The Conversation.com[1]

For decades, epidemiologists have warned of the risks of new pandemics in our world of stressed natural environments, densely populated cities and global travel networks. The history of the relationship between cities, the environment and disease shows that cities and civilizations have always been vulnerable to the rapid spread of infections: what the ancients called plagues.

While societies often rebounded from such catastrophes, outbreaks set the stage for subsequent social and political change. For instance, plague during the third century helped undermine the Roman Empire not only by decimating the population but also by weakening the economic, cultural and religious underpinnings of urban and state structures.

As recovering Romans increasingly converted to Christianity, they refused to contribute to maintaining temples and fountains associated with pagan gods. Grand cities began to decline.

In the 14th century, the Black Death killed a third to a half of Europeans. In the aftermath, towns that in previous years had expanded their walls to accommodate growth found themselves with open space that Renaissance aristocrats and their urban designers subsequently transformed into parks, urban squares and promenades that now grace the great cities of Europe.

How recovery built cities

Waves of epidemics following European contact in the 15th century devastated cultures across the Americas, leaving towns emptied and sophisticated knowledge lost.

Cholera and other outbreaks in the crowded and unsanitary cities of the 19th century led not only to major sanitary reforms but to the institutionalization of public health measures and town planning practices. The desire for ventilation and daylight that Victorian-era epidemics reinforced influenced the streets, parks, urban spaces and homes we planned and built through the 20th century.

History reminds us that civilizations and cities create the conditions within which diseases rise and spread; pandemics in return can change important features of cities and civilizations.

Cities challenged by the pandemic

In his 1912 pamphlet "Nothing gained from overcrowding", the British town planner Raymond Unwin advocated a maximum of 12 houses per acre. By the 1990s, the planning preference for relatively low urban densities, which contributed to sprawl and suburbanization, was replaced in many Western nations with policies encouraging high densities, mixed use and transit-oriented development thought to enhance the efficiency of infrastructure and services.

The current pandemic challenges contemporary planning prescriptions for urban livability and economic vitality. Cities face significant risks during density-susceptible epidemics, with numbers of cases and death rates linked to population density and city size.

Many cities have closed the green spaces intended to provide recreation for the residents of dense neighbourhoods, leaving home-bound residents of small units feeling trapped, especially if they have children to keep active and engaged. The poorest urban residents lack adequate shelter and sanitation to stay safe and socially distanced.

Essential transit systems, often feared as nodes and corridors for virus spread, are operating below capacity. Mixed-use zones with concentrations of cafes, fitness studios and restaurants are struggling to survive as the "third places" valued for social interaction have had to go virtual.

Higher death rates among racialized populations and racist attacks against Asian residents threaten planning's commitment to diversity and integration. The usual strategies for designing cities may need to be reconsidered.

What can cities learn from lockdown?

What lessons can cities draw from this crisis to inform future planning? We may need to reconsider the push for higher urban densities. Crowded housing increases contagion risks.

After being cooped up in towers for months on end, urban dwellers may begin to look at suburban lots more longingly than they did in past: living preferences may change. Everyone needs some access to outside space for mental health and exercise. We may want to consider broader park paths or longer benches that enable physical distancing, or better strategies for managing who uses space when. Those who can walk to work or to shop are appreciating that ability during these times, but we need to ensure that more have that choice.

The pandemic has brought inequality into stark relief. Everyone needs a living income to keep us all safe. Governments need to plan decent housing for all, not only for social justice reasons but for public health.

Although it's too early to predict the long-term impacts of the pandemic on our cities, our societies and ourselves, we know that things will never be quite the same again. We need to learn the lessons of our current difficulties and plan effectively to meet the challenges ahead.

Notes

1. Jill L Grant, 28 April 2020. ""What cities can learn from lockdown about planning for life after the coronavirus pandemic" https://theconversation.com/what-cities-can-learn-from-lockdown-about-planning-for-life-after-the-coronavirus-pandemic-136699